November

Dear Robin

Thanks for
all your
Kind
thoughts
&
words

Love
Linda

Presented to

_____

On the Occasion of

_____

From

_____

Date

_____

IN THE GARDEN

A Collection of Prayers for Everyday

MARSHA MAURER

PROMISE PRESS

An Imprint of Barbour Publishing

ISBN 1-57748-742-7

Published by Barbour Publishing, Inc., P. O. Box 719, Uhrichsville, Ohio 44683
http://www.barbourbooks.com

Member of the
Evangelical Christian
Publishers Association

Printed in China.

IN THE GARDEN

A Collection of Prayers for Everyday

Dedication

To my parents,
who instilled my love for God and the garden,
and to my husband,
who teaches me about heartfelt prayer.

Garden Objects

HOE

A Prayer to Weed My Faults

Hoeing is hard, exhausting work. Where do these weeds come from anyway? They weren't here earlier, and now suddenly they are choking my garden.

These weeds are like the little faults I fail to see until they grow into troublesome failures, offenses that distress me and injure others. Lord, help me to recognize my defects; I want to grow Your Spirit's fruit, not my stubborn sins. Uproot my self-centeredness, my inability to compromise, my judgmental attitude, my thoughtless insensitivity. Remove my dissatisfaction, my greed, my misguided priorities. Clear the ground to make room for the growth of a patient, generous spirit. Make me the blessing You intended when You planted me. Amen.

"The worries of this life, the deceitfulness of wealth
and the desires for other things come in
and choke the word, making it unfruitful."

Mark 4:19

GLOVES

A Prayer for Meeting a Challenge

Help me to get a grip, God. I need to pull on the comfortable, well-worn gloves Your grace so dependably supplies. Give me confidence in my ability; assure me that I can do this difficult job. Let me get a good grip on this task, so I can accomplish this work You've given me. Help me pick up the gauntlet and meet this challenge. Amen.

"Your right hand, O LORD, was majestic in power."

Exodus 15:6

RAKE

A Prayer for Dealing with Others

As a rake combs the soil, God, smooth the surface of my interactions with others. Help me to be friendly, to inspire confidence, to find the things we have in common. Show me how to seek the good in others, to refrain from criticism, to offer praise and gratitude. Teach me to be fair in my dealings, calm in disagreement, ready to compromise, and quick to apologize. Give me good humor to level the rough spots, and prepare my ground for fruitful relationships. Amen.

"Be kind and compassionate to one another, forgiving each other, even as in Christ God forgave you."

Ephesians 4:32

SHOVEL

A Prayer for Our Country

Our nation's prosperity began with shovels, God. It took hard work and the courageous lives of many before us to build homes, to plant crops, to establish lives and government.

We say we love our country, God, but are we willing to work to maintain our nation's liberties? We say we value representative government, but in how many elections do we vote? We say we value democratic process, but how informed are we about local, state, and national issues? We say we value freedom of speech, but how often do we express our views to elected officials or to local media? We say we value education, but how often do we participate in the activities of nearby schools? We say we value justice, but how often do we try to evade jury duty?

May we see the importance of exercising our love for our country. Give wisdom and sound judgment to our officials, our press, our educators, our law enforcement officers, our armed forces. Encourage us to participate in our government. Let us dig in to sustain the freedoms we enjoy. Amen.

"Blessed is the nation whose God is the LORD,
the people he chose for his inheritance."
Psalm 33:12

SHEERS

A Prayer to Shape My Life

Keep snipping, God.
Prune my weedy excesses,
my straggling imperfections,
my lop-sided selfishness. Remove
any branches that impinge on others; trim
the disorder from my life. Fashion me in the image of Your perfection. Shape my life into
a balanced, pleasing form. Amen.

"He who began a good work in you will carry it
on to completion until the day of Christ Jesus."

Philippians 1:6

WHEELBARROW
A Prayer for Help Bearing Burdens

How can I move this pile of troubles, God? How can I carry this load of worry? I can't budge it, Lord; my strength is just too weak. I need Your roomy wheelbarrow—big enough to haul all my problems, dependable enough to bear all my distress—to lug away these heavy burdens. Remove my cares—and replace them with a new load of help and hope. Amen.

"Cast your cares on the LORD, and he will sustain You."

Psalm 55:22

FERTILIZER

A Prayer on Being a Blessing to Others

Make me a blessing to those with whom I live and associate, God. Encourage me to fertilize others with the vitality that You produce in my own life. By a word of kindness, an act of generosity, let me show those around me Your luxuriant love. By turning away a hurtful word, by a positive approach, let me share Your generative power. By recognizing a need, by lending unsolicited support, may I spread Your life-giving force. May all those I encounter grow in Your plentiful grace. Amen.

*As I have loved you,
so you must love one another.*

John 13:34

BASKET

A Prayer of Thanksgiving

My basket overflows, God, with Your generous bounty. Thank You for the promise of opportunity and the comfort of security. Thank You for meaningful relationships, satisfying work, and healthy strength. Thank You for the delight of knowledge and the fulfillment of ability. Thank You for pleasant anticipation, present joy, and fond reflection. Thank You for Your abiding presence. How you load my life with blessing! Amen.

"Give thanks to the LORD, for he is good. His love endures forever."

Psalm 136: 1

WEATHERVANE

A Prayer to Seek God

Let me turn to You at all points of my life, God. . . .

From the north. . .when in need, may I invoke Your name.
Nourish, nurture, and renew me.

To the south. . .when feeling self-sufficient, may I remember to
serve You still and seek Your will.

To the east. . .when I err, may I quickly entreat You to bring me
back to Your path. Enable me to follow You.

To the west. . .when I wonder at my well-being and all the miracles
around me, may I worship Your providence and perfect wisdom.

May the currents of my life always point in prayer to You. Amen.

"Ask and it will be given to you; seek and you will
find; knock and the door will be opened to you."
Matthew 7:7

> *"My heart is glad and my tongue rejoices; my body also will rest secure."*
>
> Psalm 16:9

RAIN GAUGE

A Prayer for Optimism

Is my rain gauge half empty, God, or half full? Make me optimistic! May I find excitement, rather than fear, in opportunity; potential growth, rather than catastrophe, in disappointment. May I find compromise, rather than conflict, in disagreement; gratitude, rather than regret, in loss. May I find renewal, rather than disturbance, in change; patience, rather than defeat, in delay. Encourage me to see that if I expect the best, I shall often achieve it. Give me a positive measure of hope. Amen.

SUNDIAL

A Prayer to Bless My Hours

In the day ahead, God, my life awaits me. How shall I use all those hours around the sundial? Light my life, its countless feelings, thoughts, and actions, with the sunshine of Your grace. May every moment be inspired by Your mercies in the past, celebrated by Your presence in the present, and motivated by Your promise for the future. Bless my days with a vision of eternity. Amen.

"Keep watch, because you do not know on what day your Lord will come."

Matthew 24:42

BIRDHOUSE

A Prayer for Contentment

How happy the birds are with their plain, small birdhouse! They need none of the fine adornments I seem to think a home requires. How many trappings I need, how much accumulation of possessions. Satisfy me simply, God. Make me less acquisitive. Let me know the pleasures of modest living. Remind me that my stuck windows, unpaid bills, and stubborn children mean light to shine, blessing to enjoy, family to love. I thank You for my home. Make Your perch on my heart, God, and fill me with a song of contentment. Amen.

"Be content with what you have."

Hebrews 13:5

WIND CHIMES

A Prayer for Harmony

No matter how preoccupied I am, Lord, the clear, sweet tinkling of the wind chimes makes me pause while I silently listen to Your presence in my life. Like the summons of church bells, the wind chimes prompt me to meditate on Your goodness and grace. They remind me to live my life in harmony with You. Tune me to Your ways, Lord, so my life will resound with heaven's music. Amen.

"Blessed is the people that
know the joyful sound:
*they shall walk, O L*ORD,
in the light
of thy countenance."

Psalm 89:15 KJV

GAZING GLOBE

A Prayer in Praise of God's Goodness

In the gazing globe's reflection I see a glimpse of God's perfect original garden. Paradise shines in the shimmering sphere, whole, sublime, and right. As I walk around the globe, I see Your supreme pattern in the relation and balance of Your world, God. All is ordered, connected, ordained by Your transcendent imagination. Help me to also be a reflection of Your excellence. Amen.

"The LORD is good and his love endures forever; his faithfulness continues through all generations."

Psalm 100:5

SWING

A Prayer for Courtesy

Dealing with those around me is not always easy. Sometimes I need to pump hard as I swing between myself and another. May I be affable and courteous in the push and pull of social exchange; amiable and polite in the back and forth of business enterprise; respectful and kind in the give and take of family interaction. Make me attentive to the needs and desires of others, as I would have them be to me. Oil our squeaking differences, and keep our communication swinging freely. May I move courteously among others, God. Amen.

"Love your neighbor as yourself."

Matthew 22:39

GATE

A Prayer for Worship

Through its gates, I glimpse a garden's pleasures. In the same way, a church's door reveals Your glories. May I enter Your gates often to worship while I. . .

> hear Your word explained;
> praise You for Your blessings;
> rest from the relentless world;
> heal heart, mind, and body;
> receive Your forgiveness;
> share my faith;
> pray for the suffering;
> am revived by Your Spirit;
> prepare for Your service.

I'll meet You in church, God. Amen.

"Enter his gates with thanksgiving
and his courts with praise;
give thanks to him and praise his name."

Psalm 100:4

FOUNTAIN

A Prayer to Be a Blessing to Others

From Your deep well of goodness, God, blessings rush forth, spilling generously, boundlessly into my life. Make me a fountain that splashes Your refreshing waters onto others. Let my attitude and actions overflow with the generous love from Your sacred source. May I brim over with Your virtue and charity; may Your selflessness and forgiveness stream from me. Well up in me and spring forth in cascades of grace that will renew others with Your life-giving water. Amen.

"To him who is thirsty I will give to drink without cost from the spring of the water of life."

Revelation 21:6

Garden Creatures

BEES

A Prayer for Industry

I need the industry of bees, God, if I am to manage all my duties. When I flit from task to task, I seldom give my best. Keep me focused, devoted to the endeavor before me. Make me persistent and diligent, even in the face of tedious chores. Improve my performance by improving my attitude. Keep me from droning about, worrying, waiting for others to do the job. Make me enterprising and resourceful. Give me the skill I need to be competent, the energy I need to be efficient, the purpose I need to be effective. Sustain my momentum. Make me not just occupied, but engaged; not just active, but productive. And when I am done, may the products of my work be sweet as honey. Amen.

"A woman who fears the LORD is to be praised. Give her the reward she has earned, and let her works bring her praise at the city gate."

Proverbs 31:30–31

BIRDS

A Prayer for the family

God, give our households the same sweet harmony I hear in the birds' songs. Stabilize and strengthen our families. Restore the sanctity of marriage. Let parents demonstrate a respect and love for each other that children may imitate. Keep us from indulging our children, confusing material excess with spiritual necessity. Soothe the occasional ruffled feathers, and teach us to live in blessed concert. Amen.

"Look at the birds of the air; they do not sow or reap or store away in barns, and yet your heavenly Father feeds them. Are you not much more valuable than they?"

Matthew 6:26

THE CATERPILLAR AND THE BUTTERFLY

A Prayer for Acceptance

Remind me, God, that the fat, squirmy caterpillar gorging in my garden will soon be a lovely butterfly. How easy it is to judge others by appearance, gender, or social class, even when I chafe against being categorized myself by the preconceptions of others.

Forgive my shortsightedness, my prejudices. Let me allow others the same opportunities to express their individuality that I desire for myself. Help me to see the beauty and benefit in diversity. You do not discriminate; Your creation demonstrates how vital variety is to the functioning of our complex universe. May I seek to see the value and blessing in each of Your creatures. Amen.

"So in Christ we who are many form one body,
and each member belongs to all the others."

Romans 12:5

SQUIRRELS

A Prayer for Enthusiasm

Lord, may I, like the whirling, twirling
squirrels, be energized with zest and
zip and zeal. Ban the gloomy dol-
drums from my heart. Spark me
with spirit and spunk. Rev me
with vim and vigor and verve.
Thrill me with the prospect of
the next high branch. Amen.

*"Serve
the LORD
with
gladness."*

Psalm 100:2

SPIDERS

A Prayer for Patience

How persistently Your spider spins its web,
God, ready to enfold that which will nourish.
Teach me by the spider's patience while I
wait. . .in snarled traffic, in doctors' offices, in
crawling shopping lines. Help me to work
steadfastly at routine tasks under daily stress, to
endure the struggle, to tolerate frustration, to
meet obligation, to persevere though I am exhausted.
Help me to bear adversity, to persist in the face of hardship, to push past the disappointment, to keep going when I
would like to quit. Let me lean on You. Assure me that in my longest hours, You will listen and understand and respond. Remind me that Your web of intricately spun promises
will sustain me always. Amen.

"We also rejoice in our sufferings,
because we know that suffering produces perseverance;
perseverance, character; and character, hope."

Romans 5:3–4

FROGS AND TOADS

A Prayer for Perspective

When we think of it, Lord, frogs and toads and horny creatures are not so unsightly in their place. As with much we find distasteful in our lives, their appearance is a matter of perspective.

Are the trivial vexations really so bothersome, the small crises truly so troubling, the momentary annoyances actually so distressing? Remind us that life is often untidy, inaccurate, inconvenient, unfinished. Give us the long view, the perspective of time. Show us that our lives are shaped by what we choose to emphasize. Keep us from dwelling on the inconsequential. Make us mindful of what truly matters. Remind us that how we view the world is how the world views us. Amen.

"Do not conform any longer to the pattern of this world, but be transformed by the renewing of your mind. Then you will be able to test and approve what God's will is—his good, pleasing and perfect will."

Romans 12:2

CRICKETS

A Prayer to Recognize God's Presence

You are always there, God, letting me know You are near, Your voice as soft and steady as a cricket's chirping. I hear You in Your Word, in my answered prayers, in the concern of others. You are there in miraculous nature, in the ordered world, in the logic of reason. You are there in the right choice, in the appropriate word, in the successful effort. You are there in deliverance from danger, in failure redeemed, in health recovered, in a relationship restored. I am safe and sound in Your presence. All through the night, I can hear Your song in the dark. Amen.

" Surely I will be with you always, to the very end of the age."

Matthew 28:20

LIGHTNING BUGS

A Prayer to Help Someone Suffering

In the dusk, lightning bugs appear, God, bright and unexpected. In the same way, may I illuminate the dark hour of another's suffering. When it is easier to avoid or to withdraw, help me to reach out to the person who is bitter, angry, frustrated, or hurt. Let me listen patiently to the uncomfortable rage, complaint, and tears. Help me to understand, encourage, and reassure. In tangible ways, may I offer help and express the glow of Your love. Help me to share the glimmering evidence of Your guidance, strength, and delivery in my own difficulties. Remind me of the power of prayerful intercession to dispel gloom. Make me a brilliant flash of Your presence. Amen.

"Let your light shine before men,
that they may see your good deeds,
and praise your Father in heaven."

Matthew 5:16

A Prayer for Pets

Thank you for the beloved animals who share our homes and lives, God. They demand so little—a word, a pat, a bowl of food. But they give us so much—soothing warmth, loyal company, and unconditional affection. Keep them well and keep them from harm. Take care of those strays and castaways who have no home, those who are lost, or sick, or dying. Remind us of our responsibilities to Your creatures. May we return their love and devotion with faithful care and gentle kindness. Amen.

" And God created. . . every living creature. . . and God saw that it was good."

Genesis 1:21 KJV

LADYBUGS

A Prayer in Anticipation of Heaven

Keep us mindful of our heavenly home, God. The lady bug of the nursery rhyme who is exhorted to "fly away home" reminds us of the fulfillment of Your promises. As we face the trials of this world, make us aware of our purpose here to serve and grow. Keep us from feeling satisfied with a static spirituality. May we seek to demonstrate Your grace and to mature in our faith until Your work in our lives is complete. Then take us to the home You have prepared for us. Amen.

"In my father's house are many mansions. . . I go to prepare a place for you."

John 14:2 KJV

EARTHWORMS

A Prayer for Grace

The lowly worm transforms the earth, God. Burrowing and casting, it aerates and fertilizes the soil. So You, in Your humble incarnation as man, transformed the world. You offer to fill us with faith and to redeem us with forgiveness. Though we desperately require Your grace, we are reluctant. Our pride and prosperity impede us. Yet You steadfastly extend Your love, lavishly and unconditionally. Make us recognize our need. Sanctify, enrich, and transform us by Your divine grace. Amen.

"God resisteth the proud but giveth grace to the humble."

James 4:6

Garden World

DEW

A Prayer for Reconciliation

Send Your dew, God, to soothe our disagreement. Cleanse us of resentment and self-absorption. Help us to resolve our discord by listening attentively with genuine interest. May I set aside my own opinions and agenda so that I can hear with an open mind. If I am impatient, interrupting to contradict, I can never truly understand. Teach me to forgive. Reconcile our differences. Restore our mutual respect. Shed the life-giving moisture of Your mercy to revive our relationship. Amen.

"Love your enemies, bless them that curse you,
do good to them that hate you,
and pray for them which despitefully use you,
and persecute you;
That ye may be the children of your
Father which is in heaven."

Matthew 5:44–45 KJV

EARTH

A Prayer in Praise of Life

You are the genesis of life, God. From You, all creation is formed. The fertile world springs from Your immortal depths; all being grows from You. You quicken nature and make it fruitful. And when our time is fulfilled, You return us to dust to revive the soil below, and give us new life above. Bless the ground by which we live. Amen.

"The LORD God formed man from the dust of the ground, and breathed into his nostrils the breath of life, and man became a living being."

Genesis 2:7

SUNRISE

A Prayer for New Babies

Your rising sun beams brightly, God, on this new child. Fulfill his early promise. Light his life with health. Brighten his life with joy. Illuminate his life with wisdom. Warm his life with peace. Teach him the splendor of Your precepts. Make his future blaze with Your divine devotion. Shine on this little one and make him Your radiant child. Amen.

"Let the little children come to me, and do not hinder them, for the kingdom of God belongs to such as these."

Mark 10:14

SHADE

A Prayer of Thanks for Peace

After the world's bright glare, God, Your shade is welcome. Thank You for relief from clamor when the world is too noisy, for respite from confusion when the world is too fast, for rest from weariness when the world is too full, for release from overload when the world is too much. Cover us with Your veil of peace. Amen.

"Peace I leave with you; my peace I give unto you:
not as the world giveth, give I unto you.
Let not your heart be troubled, neither let it be afraid."

John 14:27 KJV

CLOUDS

A Prayer for a Positive Perspective

Why do we complain so much about cloudy days, God? Would we recognize the splendor of endless sunshine? When towering dark obstacles loom to block Your light, help me to see the promise in disappointment, the reward in hardship, the benefit in affliction. When wisps of difficulty persist in diffusing Your rays, remind me of the blessing in distress, the gain in loss. On dark days, may I seek Your silver lining. Amen.

"Your love, O LORD, reaches to the heavens,
Your faithfulness to the skies."

Psalm 36:5

WIND

A Prayer for Adapting to Change

Change is difficult, God. Suddenly the wind shifts directions, pushing me one way, pulling me another. My routine is disturbed, my comfort assaulted. Deviating from the familiar and predictable makes me anxious. I cling to convention and hesitate before the unknown. Rooted in habit, I resist the new and different. Make me flexible, supple, receptive to revision. Let me see that in accommodating to new experiences, I can become more responsive, capable, and confident. Make me open, expectant, and ready. Blow the dust and cobwebs from my life. Sweep me with the breath of Your renewing Spirit. Amen.

"Those who hope in the LORD
will renew their strength.
They will soar on
wings like eagles."

Isaiah 40:31

STORM

A Prayer in Trouble, Despair, Fear, or Pain

Storms tear and howl about me, God. I am afraid and desperate. Comfort and empower me through this turbulence. Assure me that all during this trial, You will hold me close. In these difficult hours when I feel cursed and alone, remind me that You will watch with me. In these dark moments when I feel confused, angry, and impatient, help me to see beyond the tumult to clearer skies. Remind me that through the suffering of Your own Son, You can understand my pain; You will not test me beyond my endurance. Give me the patience and perseverance I need until the sun returns. Amen.

> *"They cried out to the Lord in their trouble, and he brought them out of their distress. He stilled the storm to a whisper; the waves of the sea were hushed."*
>
> Psalm 107:28–29

PUGGLES

A Prayer to Appreciate Life's Messes

Life is messy, God. Sometimes I imagine how easy life would be without all the mud puddles in my path—the interruptions, the difficulties, other people's feelings to consider, schedules to meet, aggravations that just seem to get in the way of what I wish to accomplish. I need to be reminded of how much fun puddles are to the child who encounters life with joyful delight. The unexpected people, the unscheduled opportunities, the unplanned occurrences need not deter my plans; instead, they can enrich my life with the joy of surprise. Help me to give myself permission to change my mind, to see things in new ways, to enjoy the complexity of Your creation. And thank You for the puddles that keep me from becoming inflexible. Amen.

"And we know that in all things God works for the good of those who love him."

Romans 8:28

RAIN

A Prayer in Time of Spiritual Drought

I am in a dry spell, God. While weeds of neglect thrive, do not let my spirituality wither. Pour down Your rain to perk up my drooping faith. Quench my thirst with Your Word. Soak through my hard heart, so that Your life may seep into my parched soul. Shower me with the cool, vital refreshment of Your Spirit. Amen.

"The Lord will guide you always;
he will satisfy your needs in a sun-scorched land. . .
You will be like a well-watered garden,
like a spring whose waters
never fail."

Isaiah 58:11

RAINBOW

A Prayer Recalling God's Promises

A radiant vision of Your promises unfurls across Your firmament, God, a vivid reminder of Your enduring vows. Here is Your glorious pledge to us, arching across the heavens, a celestial flag assuring us that Your promises are real and true and lasting. How spectacular is Your smile. Thank You for this bright banner, the broad spectrum of Your covenant. Amen.

"I have set my rainbow in the clouds, and it will be the sign of the covenant between me and the earth."

Genesis 9:13

"Teach me knowledge and good judgment
for I believe in your command."

Psalm 119:66

FIRE

A Prayer to Take Responsibility

Temper me in Your fire, God, so that I may accept responsibility. Kindle me so that I will be inspired to fulfill my obligations and answer for my behavior. Keep me from smoldering with resentment, blaming others, feeling victimized. May I use good judgment to make rational, moral decisions. Make me burn with accountability. Amen.

ICICLES

A Prayer to Simplify Life

Drip by soundless drip, God, Your jeweled icicles
grow to dazzling lengths. Give my life the same
serene splendor. . .a gentle tempo, a quiet light.
Let me hear the silent hush between life's rush
and push. Keep me from wasting time regretting
what was or worrying about what will be, but
instead, teach me to accept and appreciate what is.
I want to absorb the moment just past, savor the
one in progress, and prepare for the one ahead.
Help me to reduce the urgency that crowds my life.
Give me a deeper participation in fewer activities. Let
me find a comfortable balance between motion and rest,
moving slowly with the rhythm of the day. I ask You to
give me relaxing interludes for insight, calm pauses to drift and
replenish, quiet moments of closer communion with Your natural world. Make my life
shimmer with simplicity. Amen.

"Do not worry about tomorrow,
for tomorrow will worry about itself."

Matthew 6:34

A Prayer for Awareness of God

Like your frosty filigree on glass, God, You form the patterns of our lives. Too often we fail to heed the evidence of Your presence. Like Mary at the tomb and the disciples on the way to Emmaus, we do not recognize Your nearness. Give us clarity of vision that we may see Your closeness through portals which may seem icily obscured. Thaw our frozen sensibilities. Open our sight to Your appearance in our lives' design. Amen.

"Then their eyes were opened, and they recognized Him."

Luke 24:31

SUNSET

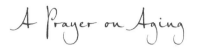

A Prayer on Aging

In brilliant serenity, the sun goes down; may my late hours be as radiant, God. Make me responsive to new people, activities, and ideas, that I may continue to learn and grow. Keep me from imposing my judgment on others. Remind me that we each must learn from our own experiences. Relieve my fears and frustrations. Keep me from dwelling on my limitations and losses. Instead, help me find a suitable pace to engage in what I can, more thoughtfully and fully. Let me enjoy the rewards of the moment, the pleasures of looking ahead. And when my life sinks into eternity at last, may I leave this world aglow with grace. Amen.

"Thine age shall be clearer than the noonday; thou shalt shine forth, thou shalt be as the morning."

Job 11:17 KJV

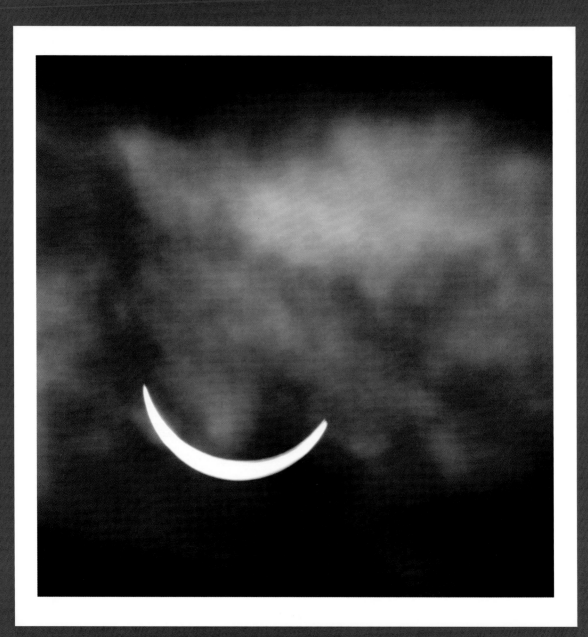

MOON

A Prayer for Righteousness

Make me like the moon, a reflection of Your Son's perfect righteousness. As Christ accepted His humanity, His poverty, His degradation, make me obedient. As He refused to sin, make me pure. As He bore indignity and injustice, pain and suffering, make me patient. As He forgave those who persecuted and killed Him, make me forgiving. As He believed Your promises, make me trusting. As the moon returns the sun's light to us throughout the night's darkness, may my life reflect Your glory to the world. Amen.

"Create in me a clean heart, O God; and renew a right spirit within me."

Psalm 51:10 KJV

STAR

A Prayer for Perseverance

Make me see my dreams come true, God—not by wishing on a star, but by working purposefully and steadily toward my goals. Those sparks in the night firmament glow with the illusion of instant and spontaneous brightness. But in fact, long before I perceived their glimmer, they have been light years in the shining.

So it is with my ambitions. Remind me that results are seldom observable overnight, that long effort with passionate intensity is the most dependable means of achievement. As I strive, give me pleasure in the routine. Just as You led the magi to Your extraordinary revelation, guide me and keep me on task. Crown my perseverance with success. Amen.

"We have seen his star in the East and are come to worship him."

Matthew 2:2 KJV

Garden Plants

SEED

A Prayer for Purpose

A seed holds the complete design for life: The plan becomes the plant. In the same way, Lord, let me see Your purpose contained in my life. Although I often flounder and struggle to find direction, I know that my existence is not by accident or chance. Remind me of Your intention for my life. I am not here for pleasure, honor, prestige, or wealth. Guide me to see that selfish enjoyment is not Your aim for me. Make my life a blessing to others. May the seed that You planted in my heart at my creation grow to maturity. Whether conditions be fertile or barren, make me bloom with the deeply planted satisfaction of Your will. Amen.

"These are they which are sown on good ground; such as hear the word, and receive it, and bring forth fruit."

Mark 4:20

SEED PODS

A Prayer for Protection

Enfolded in their pods, seeds are kept safe. Keep us as secure, God. Protect us from injury, illness, and peril. Preserve us from crisis, turmoil, and despair. Defend us from vice, temptation, and evil. Keep us sheltered in Your care. Amen.

"Whoever listens to me will live in safety and be at ease, without fear of harm."

Proverbs 1:33

ROOTS

A Prayer for Commitment

Make me rooted, God. Keep me from involving myself in so many activities that I cannot give my best. Direct me to those people and efforts that are truly important. May I concentrate my time more wholly, dedicate my talents more fully, devote my energy more diligently, and focus my attention more completely. Reward my deeper engagement with greater fulfillment. May my roots always draw their nourishment from Your life. Amen.

"Commit your way to the LORD;
trust in him and he will do this:
He will make your righteousness
shine like the dawn, the
justice of your cause like
the noonday sun."

Psalm 37:5

STEMS

A Prayer for Confidence

A slender stem supports both leaf and flower. God, give me the same strength to bear my responsibilities. Make me confident in my skill and talent. Help me to develop my competence. Make me resourceful and resilient. Assure me that I can excel. Give me courage to rise to my challenges, and make me flourish. Amen.

"The Lord shall be thy confidence."

Proverbs 3:26

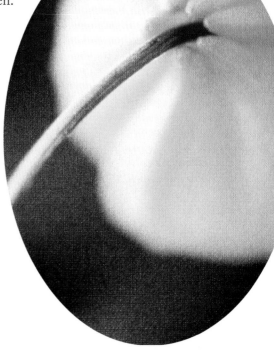

GRASS

*A Prayer of Gratitude
for the Commonplace*

We seldom notice Your grass, God. It is simply there, normal, unremarkable, like much of our day-to-day activity. Thank You for routine, for the regularity of the commonplace. In our often chaotic and fragmented lives, the familiar reassures us. When duty grows wearisome, remind us that much can be accomplished simply through deliberate and habitual repetition. Thank You for this opportunity to appreciate the ordinary. Amen.

*"If that is how God clothes the grass of the field,
which is here today
and tomorrow is thrown into the fire,
will he not much more clothe you,
O you of little faith?"*

Matthew 6:30

LEAVES

A Prayer on Praying

In the leaves of plants, light is transformed into food and oxygen. God, may my prayers be equally energized. Make prayer a natural part of my life, that I may speak to You with my eyes open, without prescribed motions or postures.

Remind me that I can talk to You out loud or silently in my own words whenever I wish, wherever I am. Encourage me to express my joy and gratitude as well as my concern and fear. Assure me that You are listening even if I cannot know or understand Your response. Empower my prayer with the light of Your Spirit, so that I will yield nourishment and life to those around me. Amen.

"If you believe, you will receive whatever you ask for in prayer."

Matthew 21:22

FRAGRANT FLOWERS

A Prayer to Use My Gifts

The lily, lilac, and lemon flower each smells distinctively fragrant. In a similar way, Lord, You have anointed my life with its own aroma. May Your gifts flower fully in me, giving off Your pleasing perfume. Let me use my talents and abilities that others may know You by the sweet scent of Your pervading goodness. Amen.

> ## *"They may see your good deed*
> ## *and glorify God."*
>
> 1 Peter 2:12

VINES

A Prayer in Caring for Children

How quickly Your vines grow, God. Soon small plantings are leaping, reaching, searching for new ground to cling to, for new places to flourish. They remind me of the children in my care. Young ones who now embrace me will soon be stretching and pushing their own boundaries.

Keep me responsible and loving as I train their growth. Help me to be sensitive to their tender feelings, to reassure them when they are fearful, to give them my time generously and willingly. Help me to respect their own thoughts and ideas, to answer their endless questions, to listen genuinely. Help me to allow them freedom to make their own decisions, that they may learn from consequences. Help to give them the security of firm guidance, to say no when necessary, to be consistent and fair. May I hold them accountable, and hold them close.

Help me to allow for mistakes and imperfection as they grow and explore, to build confidence with sincere praise, to delight in their achievement. Help me to be slow to anger, to apologize when I err, to live a good example. Help me to laugh with them, pray for them, and trust them to Your care. Show me how best to help Your dear children through their growing pains. Amen.

> *"Train a child
> in the way he should go,
> and when he is old
> he will not turn from it."*
>
> Proverbs 22:6

TREES

A Prayer for Self-Acceptance

Help me to accept myself, Lord. Turn my focus from what is wrong with me to all that is inherently right with me. Keep me from judging myself by the standards of others. Let me use the energy I expend in criticizing my faults for trusting my skills instead. Let me find the value in the unique individual You have made me. Help me to reach my potential by amplifying my good qualities, shedding my weaker traits in the process. Let me stretch my strong, resilient branches toward You that I may grow into the impressive individual You have ordained. Make me majestic, God, like a tree. Amen.

"He is like a tree
planted by streams of water,
which yields its fruit in season
and whose leaf does not wither.
Whatever he does prospers."

Psalm 1:3

Garden Bouquets

JOY

Delightful Lord,

Make me cheerful, make me playful, make me laugh out loud! What rich blessings You offer, what satisfying joy! Show me the pleasures You provide, the glories You promise.

Remind me that life is most precious now, in the present moment, rather than in the someday far ahead. Let me be open to spontaneity, serendipity, and surprise. Awake, aware, may I surrender to the delight of each moment. Give me energy, enthusiasm, and satisfaction in my work. Instead of squandering my days in acquisition, let me embrace contentment. Help me to see the opportunity in difficulty, to forget regret, and to find fun in my foibles.

For happiness is like manna raining down at my door, and all I must do is pick it up. Make me smile, Lord! Amen.

"You will fill me with joy in your presence, with eternal pleasures at your right hand."

Psalm 16:11

Chrysanthemum—Cheerfulness
Gardenia—Joy
Larkspur—Levity
Oregano—Happiness
Salad Burnet—A Merry Heart
Sweet Marjoram—Mirth

WISDOM

Omniscient Lord,

You have created us in Your image with a perfect knowledge of truth

and righteousness. But our human imperfection often clouds our vision of what is right and just and necessary. Illuminate our lives with Your wisdom. Give us a clear standard of virtue. May we be prudent as we determine our priorities, sensible as we make our judgments. Let us use our intellect and insight to make the choices and decisions that face us.

Life is rarely predictable or dependable. Teach us to recognize that change is life's only constancy. Fill our thoughts with not only precision and clarity, but also imagination. Help us not to be threatened by conflicting viewpoints; remind us that we learn by resolving contradictions.

Each day is an opportunity to learn about ourselves, about one another, about You, God. Let our thoughts and actions radiate integrity so that others may recognize Your reflection in us. Amen.

"The fear of the LORD is the beginning of wisdom, and knowledge of the Holy One is understanding."
Proverbs 9:10

Sage—Health
Lemon Balm—Healing,
*   Relief*
Eucalyptus—Get Well,
*   Take Care*

HEALTH

Healing Lord,

We praise You for the freedom of good health, for energy, vitality, and vigor. We often take for granted the miracle of our intricately functioning bodies—but how readily illness can narrow our focus on our physical condition.

Sustain those of us whose self-respect and enthusiasm for life have been shattered by pain and illness. Infirmity makes us impatient, irritable, fearful—but help us find in suffering the incentive to re-evaluate our lives, to reach into our depths to discover what is most valuable—far beyond our fondest transient pleasures—until we touch at last the contentment and peace that is beyond human understanding.

Restore not only our good health, but also our appreciation for well-being. May we live prudent, wholesome lives. Breathe in us Your breath of life and make us flourish. Amen.

" 'I will restore you to health and heal your wounds,' declares the LORD."

Jeremiah 30:17

> *Daisy—Simplicity*
> *Hawthorn—Contentment*
> *Madwort—Tranquillity*

PEACE

Eternal Lord,

In our frenzied efforts to pass time, save time, and be on time, we forget that our lives are measured by eternity. We hurry through work, recreation, and relationships. We are consumed by our possessions, by our demand for perfection, by overanalysis. We feel burdened by yesterday's disappointments, today's cares, and tomorrow's fears. Restless and distressed, we yearn for harmony in ourselves, our homes, our world. We need courage to flee the misguided priorities of the jangling masses.

Give us satisfaction in our efforts and contentment in our achievements. Resolve our conflicts and keep harm from us. Bless our days with balance among the physical, the intellectual, and the social. Teach us to delight in the peace of simplicity and the quiet space of solitude. May serenity bring grace and light to our relationships, slow our communication, and enrich our understanding. Help us find the tranquil center in our lives; fill us with Your holy calm. Amen.

"The LORD bless you and keep you; the LORD make his face shine upon you and be gracious to you; the LORD turn his face toward you and give you peace."

Numbers 6:24–26

MARRIAGE

Devoted Lord,

We thank You for each other. Give our marriage a glowing ardor that reflects Your own devotion to us. Scuffed and tarnished by time and trial, marriage easily becomes dulled. Polishing and restoring our relationship requires Your help.

> *Camellia—Steadfast Love*
> *Carnation—Pure and Ardent Love*
> *Holly—Domestic Happiness*
> *Ivy—Wedded Love*
> *Lavender—Devotion*
> *Orange Blossom—Marriage and Faithfulness*
> *Peony—Happy Marriage*

Forgive us for the times we see only the struggle and forget the love. Help us to remember daily to renew the joy of our friendship. Let us encourage the best in each other by uplifting and sustaining each other. Keep us living in tandem, steady in our stride.

May we grow through the sharing of our thoughts. Let us make conflicts constructive rather than destructive. Help us to recognize that each problem has more than one viable approach. Give us a sense of humor; fill our days with laughter. Remind us of the wonder of a gentle touch. Please, God, burnish our love till it gleams. Amen.

"This is my beloved and this is my friend."

Song of Solomon 5:16 KJV

STRENGTH

Mighty Lord,

In Your power and glory, You offer us abundant life. Only our doubt and despair keep us from claiming Your bountiful goodness.

Remove our anxiety from us, for we are not alone in our decisions: You are ready to help us face our tasks and choices. We need not be overwhelmed by the challenges before us when we know that Your strength will fortify us. Show us that the best way to overcome problems is to confront them with courage. Reassure us that burdens are temporary and remind us that opportunity often comes through adversity. Cheer us in our anguish, uplift us in our disappointment, soothe us in our frustration, and refresh us in our weariness.

May we learn to accept less than perfection. Help us to embrace our limitations and constraints as welcome guidance from You. Encourage us to see that sacrifice and toil teach us humility. When we submit to You, we find resilience of spirit. Amen.

"The Lord is the strength of my life;
of whom shall I be afraid?"

Psalm 27:1 KJV

CHARITY

Generous Lord,

Though I am thankless and undeserving, You give me Your love freely. Show me the blessing in such selfless giving; remind me that when I offer kindness, I fill my own emptiness. May I be cheerful, willing, and eager in my charity, courteous in my actions, and sincere in my intentions.

Forgive my prejudice and impatience. Help me to tolerate the irritation of thoughtless people. Let me silence the insult and in its place speak words of acceptance. Make me sensitive to the needs of others. Remind me that happiness is like a clump of flowers that flourishes when I divide it. Amen.

"It is more blessed to give than to receive."
Acts 20:35

Bluebell—Kindness
Elderflower—Compassion
Chamomile—Patience
Wild Grape—Charity

FRIENDSHIP

Familiar Lord,

What a divine gift is the company of a friend, for true friendship reflects our relationship with You. Our friends offer us dignity when we are foolish, forbearance when we are irritating, and understanding when we are melancholy. With a friend, conversation is meaningful, silence is comfortable, laughter is sincere. A friendship is not unchanging, but dependable; not demanding, but secure. We respect our differences and encourage growth in each other.

Thank You for the intimate communion of friends. Amen.

"A friend loves at all times."

Proverbs 17:17

GUIDANCE

Guiding Lord,

So many questions, God. So many unknowns. I don't know which

> *Heather—Protection*
> *Southernwood—Perseverance*
> *Tarragon—Stamina*

road to choose; I worry whether my choice will be the right one. But I am equally concerned about leaving behind the course I do not select. Will my chosen path ever again intersect with roads not taken?

I am uncertain about how to make my choice. Shall I rely on emotion or intellect, advice or intuition? I could use some signpost, God: Stop, Go, No Left Turn, Proceed with Caution.

And I am fearful of the road ahead. Perhaps it will be rutted, beset by adversaries, detoured, dead-ended, narrow, ill-lit, lonely. Will I have the fortitude to face these perils; will I be able to persevere or reroute as required?

Assure me that You are always my traveling companion, no matter which way I go. Steer me to choose wisely. Keep me from dwelling with regret on opportunities lost and let me not become immobilized by indecision. Encourage me when I falter and protect me from peril. And in the end, bring me safely to my eternal home. Amen.

"Yea, though I walk through the valley of the shadow of death, I will fear no evil, for thou art with me; thy rod and thy staff they comfort me."

Psalm 23:4 KJV

FORGIVENESS

Merciful Lord,

Why is it so difficult to admit my mistakes? My selfish pride blinds me to my own faults, even while I am quick to identify those of others. Show me my need for Your forgiveness, for when I am unhappy with others, often I am actually displeased with myself. Pardon my intolerance, my selfishness, my greed, my ignorance, my inertia, my discontent.

Remind me that I need to turn to You often for cleansing, for sanctity requires persistence. Thank You for Your grace when I fail. Amen.

Mint—Virtue
Moss Rose Bud—Confession
White Lily—Purity

"If we confess our sins, he is faithful
and just and will forgive us our sins
and purify us from all unrighteousness."

1 John 1:9

SLEEP

Restful Lord,

No matter how frantic my schedule, there faithfully, at the end of each day, lies blissful sleep, a respite from labor, a quiet interlude from noise. In the welcome darkness, my dreams release me from the day's hurried pressure.

How reassuring to commend myself to You who light the dark of night with moon and stars. I pray You may, I pray You might, grant me blessed sleep tonight. Amen.

"Come to me,
all you who are weary
and burdened,
and I will give you rest."
Matthew 11:28

White Poppy—Sleep

DEATH

Living Lord,

No matter when death arrives, it seems too soon. We always have so much living yet to do. Death closes the doors on plans and possibilities. Death concludes the stories we have yet to tell. For the living, the loss is wrenching, the void devastating.

And yet You console us with time's healing power. Our love endures in the solace of memories, and we cling to the same promise that comforts the dying—life everlasting. We shall be together again. We shall be with You. And the life we live then will be beyond the greatest joy we can imagine now. Our reunion is not so far away. Life will soon begin again. Amen.

> *Lily of the Valley—Return of Happiness*
> *Snowball—Thoughts of Heaven*
> *Sweet Woodruff—Eternal Life*
> *White Rose—Sadness*

"Blessed are those who mourn, for they will be comforted."

Matthew 5:4

NATURE'S BEAUTY

Beautiful Lord,

For the invocation of thunder, the canticle of rain,
For the psalm of brooks, for birds' refrain,
For the lullaby of locusts, for cicadas' vesper hush,
I thank You for beautiful sound.

For the quickening essence of impending rain,
the rich aroma of moldering leaves,
For balm of basil and savory dill,
for the pungency of evergreens,
For gardenias' perfume and carnations' spice,
for the fragrance of sweet lilies and lure of lilac,
I thank You for beautiful scent.

For dripping sweet peaches and nectar-filled honey,

110

for succulent tomatoes and hidden strawberries,
For earthy mushrooms and woodsy nuts,
   for peppery mint and sunny rosemary,
For tart crunch of apples, for bursting grapes,
   I thank You for beautiful taste.

For a cool sudden breeze or a trickling spring,
   for the sun's warmth on my hair,
For toe-squishing mud and powder-soft silt,
   for an on-coming storm's tingling air,
For a grassy caress and a cat's furry tickle, for the gold satin skin of a pear,
   I thank You for beautiful touch.

For shimmering light on water, for the silvery glint of fish,
For frosty iridescence, for a hummingbird's intricate dance,
For copper fields, and sunset's fire, for heaven's infinity,
   I thank You for beautiful sight. Amen.

Calla—Magnificent Beauty
Magnolia—Love of Nature
Stock—Lasting Beauty

FRUIT

A Prayer for Spiritual Nourishment

Nourish me, God. Feed and sustain me with Your generous hand. Replenish my spirit with worship, prayer, and Your Word that Your gifts may ripen in me and produce abundant fruit until You gather me in Your heavenly harvest. Amen.

"Be fruitful in every good work, and increasing in the knowledge of God."

Colossians 1:10 KJV